Implementing Curriculum Integration in Standards-Based Middle Schools

The Principal's Role

by
Jim Snapp

National Middle School Association
Westerville, Ohio

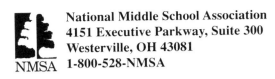

National Middle School Association
4151 Executive Parkway, Suite 300
Westerville, OH 43081
1-800-528-NMSA

NMSA is a registered servicemark of National Middle School Association. Printed in the United States of America.

Sue Swaim, Executive Director
Jeff Ward, Deputy Executive Director
April Tibbles, Director of Publications
Dawn Williams, Production Specialist
Edward Brazee, Editor, Professional Publications
John Lounsbury, Consulting Editor, Professional Publications
Mary Mitchell, Designer, Editorial Assistant
Marcia Meade-Hurst, Senior Publications Representative
Mark Shumaker, Graphic Designer

ISBN: 1-56090-191-8

CONTENTS

PREFACE

No Time to Retreat

Children are living messages we send to a time we will not see.
—John W. Whitehead

The role of the middle school principal has been evolving; once largely concerned with organizational and management issues, more and more principals are called on to lead schools instructionally (Jackson & Davis, 2000). This change takes place at a time when quantifying student learning through data analysis, balancing local and state curriculum with federal mandates, and achieving more stringent test scores have become increasingly critical.

This resource focuses on the heart of middle level education, the relationships and learning experiences that occur between students and teachers, students and students, and teachers and teachers. It reflects those deeply held beliefs that compel many educators to choose to work with young adolescents because they see the value and importance of working with these in-transition students.

Educators must ask, What are the desired outcomes for a student in our middle school? Is it to pass the state standardized test? Is it to grow as an individual? Is it to develop intellectual gifts? Is it to become a positive citizen in a democratic society? Most will agree that the ideal middle school would help achieve all these things for each of its students. If that is the case, the next question has to be, Is our curriculum structured in a way to accomplish these things? If it isn't, what must we do to prepare our students to meet these varied and desired outcomes?

Curriculum integration is a term often used by middle level educators to identify a particular approach to curriculum; however, integrated or connected curriculum has a rich history dating back to the 1890s, re-emerging with Kilpatrick's Project Method (1918) of the 1920s, and the core curriculum movement of the 1930s, '40s, and '50s. The conversation was renewed in the early 1990s as middle level educators led by James Beane, Gordon Vars, and others, expanded the curriculum integration concept to include a process centered on the concerns and questions of young adolescents. What surfaced was a model for organizing the curriculum and the emergence of truly democratic classrooms—classrooms where student voices are heard as valued parts of the learning experience. While there have always been some classrooms where integrated learning predominates, the publication of Beane's book *The Middle School Curriculum: From Rhetoric to Reality* in 1990 (with an enlarged second edition in 1993) gave educators of young adolescents both a rationale and a framework to more clearly direct their work. These educators inspired others to use these curriculum principles in a variety of instructional ways, and soon teachers around the country were sharing their experiences in what came to be called "curriculum conversations."

Central in this work is student voice, too often ignored or demeaned in the daily life of school. Young adolescents' abilities are too frequently downplayed with beliefs such as "they are too immature to really understand." Even their physical and behavioral qualities are belittled, some often referring to them as "hormones with feet." Many people, including some educators, react with signs of surprise, admiration, and occasionally disgust—"I couldn't teach middle school students"; but committed middle level educators have insights that discredit the typical stereotypes. They see young adolescents as curious, insightful, energetic, intelligent, and highly motivated learners. Through years of experiences with students these educators realize that integrating the curriculum is a highly effective way to engage students in deeper thinking and learning.

In the late 1990s the standards movement emerged and brought to a halt much of the progress made by dedicated teachers. Building administrators too often gave support to maintaining the separate subject curriculum, specialized subject-trained teachers, and rote memorization teaching practices. To be truthful, many principals who did not understand curriculum integration in the first place were happy to reaffirm the separate subject approach that characterized the junior high school. Other principals were uncomfortable with the democratic learning communities that emerged from classrooms where curriculum integration was being practiced and were pleased to see a teacher back in front of the classroom teaching from a prescribed textbook. Yet, in spite of the pressure from external mandates and traditional educators in some schools, there have remained a few brave leaders who, through their competence and convictions, continue to support and encourage curriculum integration. I hope this book will validate those progressive leaders and encourage others to assist teachers as they take up the journey toward a more coherent middle level curriculum.

TOPIC ONE

Curriculum Integration Design

Do not separate the seamless cloak of learning.
                                    –Alfred North Whitehead

Successful middle level schools have a "curriculum that is relevant, challenging, integrative, and exploratory" (National Middle School Association, 2003, p. 19). To achieve this end, the ideal middle level curriculum focuses on two closely related elements: integrated curriculum and democratic classrooms. There are several ways to organize the curriculum, ranging from a separate subject approach to a fully integrated curriculum where subject boundaries dissolve and learning activities are focused on answering authentic student questions. A second, yet equally important element of an integrated middle level curriculum is the inclusion of student voice in selecting curriculum topics, assessment measures, learning activities, and in the overall environment of the classroom, all of which result in a democratic classroom. While some would argue that absolute curriculum integration cannot take place unless both elements—curriculum integration and democratic classrooms—are fully in place, the reality is that many middle level classrooms still lack a truly democratic approach, even while making a real effort to break down strict subject boundaries.

An integrated curriculum pursues major concepts, not narrowly defined bodies of content; but in studying these concepts, all subjects are sources of pertinent information. However, no subject is the organizing center for such a curriculum; rather, a theme provides the organizing structure. Some have suggested that the different approaches to curriculum fall on a continuum that identifies the level of student involvement, teacher planning, and dissolving subject boundaries. While educators do not move methodically through each stage, the curriculum continuum serves as a point of reference for understanding various elements of the different approaches. Educators can start anywhere on the continuum and move back and forth among the ways of organizing curriculum based on each particular theme, level of expertise, and appropriateness of the curriculum approach given student learning outcomes. Beane (2002) offers excellent definitions and descriptions of four curriculum approaches in the following excerpt from *Organizing the Middle School Curriculum*, which can be found in its entirety on National Middle School Association's Web site at www.nmsa.org.

Curriculum Approaches

Separate Subject Curriculum. The separate subject curriculum is based on the concept of knowledge organized by "disciplines" or scholarly fields of specialized inquiry. Within this approach students are expected to encounter and master selected content from various disciplines through school subjects that are intended to represent them. While proponents of the separate subject approach may agree on its use as a way of organizing the curriculum, there are continuing debates over what content from particular disciplines should be included in the school curriculum and how subjects ought to be "learned.". . . The separate subject curriculum is often referred to as the "traditional" or "departmentalized" curriculum.

Multidisciplinary or Multisubject Curriculum. The multidisciplinary or multisubject curriculum is intended to correlate two or more subjects in relation to some organizing theme, concept, topic, or issue. Planning for such a curriculum usually begins with the identification of a topic or theme, followed by the question, What can various subject areas contribute to the study of the theme? In this way two concerns are addressed. First, as subjects are connected in the context of the theme or topic, they may seem less fragmented to students. Second, by opening a topic to consideration through the lenses of two or more subject areas, it may be better and more completely understood. Like the separate subject approach, the multidisciplinary or multisubject approach continues the purpose of encountering and mastering content from various subjects. Moreover, though a central theme or topic is used to correlate them, the separate subjects retain their identity and, typically, their separate time slots in the school schedule.

Interdisciplinary Curriculum. "Interdisciplinary" is a broad term used to refer to both curriculum designs and projects that seek to combine two or more disciplines of knowledge. Interdisciplinary curriculum design begins with particular disciplines and uses them to create new fields of inquiry, such as Art History or Environmental Studies, in which the individual disciplines are necessary—but not alone sufficient—for work within the new field of inquiry. In a sense, as the two examples suggest, these new fields are often close to what might be thought of as new disciplines. Interdisciplinary projects use various disciplines in combination to solve problems or consider issues that cannot be adequately addressed by any one of the disciplines alone. Interdisciplinary curriculum designs have also been referred to as "fused" or "cross-curricular."

Curriculum Integration. Curriculum integration is a curriculum design that promotes personal and social integration through the organization of curriculum around significant problems and issues, collaboratively identified by educators and young people, without regard for subject area lines. Planning for curriculum integration begins with an organizing theme followed by the question, What significant activities might be done to address the theme? Projects and other activities involve "integration" and application of knowledge in the context of a theme. Content and skills are taught, learned, and applied as they are needed to work on particular themes. While knowledge is drawn from the traditional disciplines (among other sources), students move from activity to activity, or project to project, rather than from subject to subject during the school day (as in the multidisciplinary approach). With its emphasis on real-life themes, contextual application of knowledge, and constructivist learning, the curriculum integration approach is particularly well-suited to helping students integrate learning experiences into their developing schemes of meaning. For this reason, the term "integrative" is often used to describe this approach. In one variation of curriculum integration, teachers and students plan together to create a thematic curriculum based upon questions and concerns students have about themselves and their world.

As is apparent in these definitions by Beane (2002), the level of student involvement increases as the curriculum becomes more connected. Soliciting student voice means much more than cursory input by students at the beginning of the school year over classroom management issues. Genuine student involvement is intertwined with all activities taking place in the classroom. From short-term classroom climate issues to longer-term curriculum planning, to devising assessment options, the thoughts, concerns, suggestions, and interests of young adolescents enliven the curriculum in integrative classrooms and build positive classroom learning environments.

Moving beyond multidisciplinary units

Many teams have developed multidisciplinary or interdisciplinary units of study that engage students in ways the regular curriculum rarely does; often such units are the highlight of the year for students and teachers. As successful as these units generally are, there are serious questions about how they might be even better. Could the level of coordination among teachers enhance the unit further? Could students' own interests be the focus for such units? Could boundaries between subjects be eliminated altogether to focus on larger concepts? Principals wishing to transition good thematic units into great thematic units will encourage teachers to closely examine each unit at its completion, gather feedback from students, and consider ways that it can be improved by more fully involving the students in planning and conducting the unit.

As good as most multidisciplinary units can be, they have some fundamental limitations, not the least of which is the predisposition to halt the forward progress of a team that believes it has "arrived." Multidisciplinary units are useful because they help teachers see the possibilities for greater student voice, connections across subjects, and more in-depth student thinking; but they ought not be a final destination.

QUESTIONS TO CONSIDER

- Does your current curriculum evoke real interest to and relevancy for your students?

- Does your curriculum help students to develop a positive self-image and a better understanding of the world they live in?

- Do your teachers understand the positive impact on learning that purposeful connections in the curriculum can accomplish?

- Can your teachers articulate their understanding of the curriculum models and assess the benefits that each model has to strengthen learning for young adolescents?

- How many teachers currently use the various curriculum models?

TOPIC TWO

Democratic Classrooms

*Empowerment does not seem to be an item high on our agenda.
Negative views have led us to grossly underestimate the potential
that young adolescents have to create, contribute, and assume re-
sponsibility for their own learning.*—John Arnold

*A*n effective middle level curriculum is distinguished by learning activities that appeal to young adolescents and create
opportunities to pose and answer questions that are important
to them (National Middle School Association, 2003, p.19). What is the
best way to create schools as described in this passage? Giving young
adolescents a voice in what and how they learn at this time when they
are struggling with self-identity, seeking greater autonomy, and yet
relying heavily on the opinions of others is the best time to have them
become more fully engaged in their own learning.

In democratic classrooms students have meaningful input into all
aspects of the learning experience. This input may begin with achieving agreement about classroom rules, but quickly goes beyond that
to the heart of what takes place in the classroom—learning. Beane
(1993) describes a democratic classroom as one where the curriculum is structured around the questions and concerns students have
about themselves and the world in which they live (p. 68). Based on
their questions and concerns, students identify themes and issues that
are relevant to them. From these themes, teachers and students collaboratively design learning experiences, often in a variety of ways
to demonstrate that learning, and define the expected level of student
performance or guiding rubrics. It is at the point when democratic
classrooms and curriculum integration meet that young adolescents
are in a learning environment that best matches their social, emotional,
intellectual, and physical development.

Relatively democratic classrooms can also exist in separate subject classrooms. For example, a middle level science teacher can share state standards with students, ask them what questions and concerns they have about the content, how they would like to demonstrate their learning, and even discuss assessment possibilities. A democratic classroom where students are consistently encouraged to participate is certainly more appropriate for young adolescent students than one where the teacher determines all of what students must know and how it will be learned. The classroom described above, while more engaging, still lacks the relevancy all learners crave.

A word of caution

Middle level teachers, often invigorated by a conference attended or a professional journal article read, will involve their students for the first time, seeking their input, and get dismal results. Perplexed by the lack of interest, teachers may retreat from this approach, failing to realize that students have been conditioned to a "sit and get" approach where engagement and input from students have not been sought or welcomed. Just as teachers must practice to refine their skills in this approach, so must students be exposed to more and more opportunities for meaningful input and dialogue within the classroom. Democratic classrooms demonstrate a consistent environment that is positively nurturing, encouraging, and has high expectations for student involvement and academic performance, but it has to grow to that level. Principals must be supportive of teachers and help them recognize that the long-term conditioning of students has to be considered.

Teachers in democratic classrooms understand that the culture of the classroom depends more on their behavior than anyone else's. They know that how they structure learning opportunities for students provides insights into what they value about young adolescents. Are the activities simple, dealing primarily with knowledge-based questions, using limited instructional resources, or are the learning activities complex, requiring deep thinking, causing students to extend their knowledge by talking with their classmates and experts outside the classroom, and searching a variety of sources for meaningful information? Are the learning opportunities structured to allow students to apply their knowledge in new and more complex ways?

Educators in these latter classrooms do not believe they have all the answers, and more importantly, don't believe they need to have all the answers to be effective teachers. They understand that a safe classroom environment where students feel comfortable voicing opinions, challenging answers, and stepping beyond traditional educational boundaries to provide answers is not only a stimulating place for young adolescents to learn but also a stimulating place to teach. These teachers see the classroom as a place where students learn—and where they can grow in their profession.

Curriculum Options and Level of Student Involvement

For too long many educators and citizens have viewed the middle level as a teaching wasteland—a place to hold students between elementary school and high school until they are ready to really learn again. When confronted with significant academic work that these young adolescents have produced in an integrated classroom, traditionalists are surprised to see the potential of students exemplified in various projects, speeches, essays, community service activities, and other demonstrations of in-depth learning. In response to such enlightening experiences, these once unbelieving educators will say, "I didn't believe middle school students were capable of this type of work."

Frequently when asked about how students are involved in their classrooms, teachers point to some activities where students were allowed to provide some commentary, such as helping to establish classroom rules and procedures. Other educators will claim deeper involvement pointing to such activities as K-W-L—asking students what they **K**now, what they **W**ant to know, and what they have **L**earned. A few will push student involvement further by asking students for clarifying characteristics on a scoring rubric for a particular assignment or project. Typically the range of student involvement does not move past the comfort level of the classroom teacher. Fearful of what might happen when students are given a more meaningful voice or lacking the confidence to guide student voices into learning outcomes, educators may stifle the natural interest young adolescents have for framing their own learning experiences before the desired level of engagement becomes a natural part of the classroom environment. Figure 1 illustrates that the level of student involvement increases as students move across the different types of curriculum—from separate subject to full integration.

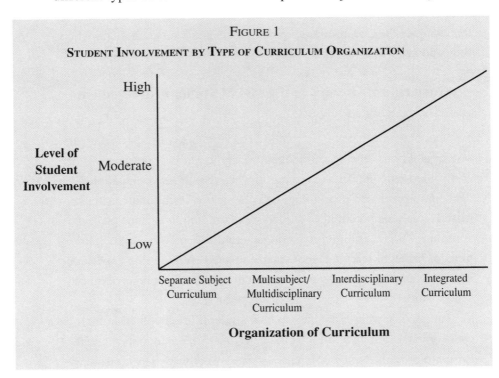

FIGURE 1

STUDENT INVOLVEMENT BY TYPE OF CURRICULUM ORGANIZATION

For those educators who are willing to take the adventurous step and give students a voice in the meatier issues of learning, the benefits often encourage them to promote even deeper, more challenging involvement of students in daily learning experiences. They find themselves incorporating state and district academic standards into questions and concerns students have raised about their world. These educators find themselves engaged in deep conversations with students on topics that were briefly "covered" in class due to a perceived shortage of time or their own reluctance and fear that students would not understand an issue in depth.

Just as the level of curriculum development tends to move from multidisciplinary to interdisciplinary to integrated curriculum, so does the level of student involvement. And while there are cases of master teachers moving directly from the single subject approach to integrated curriculum, these stories are few, as most teachers find it more comfortable to gradually allow more opportunities for student involvement.

Student involvement increases as teachers recognize that there are very few instructional issues on which students cannot provide keen input, especially when facilitated by a master teacher. Young adolescents can find the connections between seemingly unrelated content standards and also describe specific activities that allow them to demonstrate what they have learned and what specific attributes their demonstrations of learning should possess.

Creating an environment where student voice is a natural part of what takes place in the classroom involves much trial and error. While individual teachers and teams of teachers will find natural connections in the curriculum, it may take more time for these teachers to bring students into the process of assisting in the design of the learning experience and decide what will pass as evidence of deeper levels of student understanding. Likewise, other educators may involve students in rather routine and simple decisions yet struggle to allow all students to have input into the larger issues that determine the climate of the classroom or team. Experience shows that, over time, as teachers move toward truly democratic classrooms, student behavior affirms the deeply held beliefs of these educators; when given the opportunity for meaningful input into their education, students will exceed even the wisest teacher's expectations.

QUESTIONS TO CONSIDER

- How do the instructional strategies your students see provide opportunities for them to exhibit their unique gifts as learners?
- How does the curriculum promote the highest levels of thinking you want to see in your students?
- How do your students demonstrate excitement about learning?
- How do the learning experiences in your school help students to become doers? Observers?
- How are the learning environments in your classrooms inclusive and appreciative of the diversity reflected in your students and your community?

TOPIC THREE

Providing Leadership

Principal is an adjective describing a teacher; it is not a noun.
—Anonymous

The building principal plays a particularly critical role in implementing any type of integrated curriculum. It is unlikely that teams working to implement integrated curriculum will be able to sustain their effort for any period of time without the support of the principal. In schools where the inspiration for this type of work comes from classroom teachers, as it often does, the lack of a principal who supports curriculum integration can severely limit its implementation.

Effective leaders inspire teachers to courageously risk short-term failure in order to achieve success in the long run. Principals provide support in many essential areas, from scheduling to staffing, from communicating with the central office to carrying the banner of support when needed with the school board and with parents. Without a commitment from the principal, educators interested in this approach will not likely experience success.

A principal can first help teams understand the curricular options as represented along the curriculum continuum. Some teams will be ready to try integrated curriculum as their first thematic unit, while others will initially be uncomfortable with the amount of collaboration needed to accomplish a genuinely integrated unit. Others hesitate to give up the clearly defined boundaries of their designated subject areas. Principals can help teams move forward by suggesting a slight change in the time particular content or concepts are taught. By aligning the topic in this way across several different subjects, teachers and students can see the connections that exist in the curriculum. This approach is less threatening to teachers since they continue to teach the same content, but at a different time in the year. Collaboration among teachers at this stage remains very limited. The connections students make on the themes or concepts taught are implicit since the teachers do not as yet build on the strengths of each other's teaching or commonalities in content. Unfortunately many teams stagnate at this stage of development, since carrying out an interdisciplinary unit takes considerably more time, collaboration, and in many cases requires reorganizing what and when one teaches.

Encouraged by the success of a multidisciplinary unit as evidenced by student enthusiasm, teams may forge ahead with greater collaboration, moving to interdisciplinary themes and units. A common theme is identified, and teachers review content standards to see which ones naturally fit in this unit. As the standards fit into the unit, links between the content areas are extended. Teachers begin to use content knowledge shared in one class to strengthen what they are teaching in another. The curricular connections become structured, purposeful, and more explicit.

As teachers gain comfort in coordinating content, often various methods for assessing student work begin to emerge. Separate projects and other assignments are combined across subject areas allowing students to submit one project for the entire thematic unit of study. As with any good assessment, quality standards represented by a rubric are presented to the students in advance of the project.

Students may develop the levels of sophistication in the rubric. Teachers then assess the project, collaborating with students through the process of developing the curriculum, the delivery of the curriculum, and finally the assessment of student work.

One common mistake made with any curriculum format is trying to force a particular subject into a theme whether it fits or not. And another common mistake is when the unit schedule requires participating teachers to begin and end on the same day. Such a requirement is often the death knell for any type of curricular connection. All themes are not created equal! In some cases certain subjects will not fit into the theme selected. This is not a reason to avoid the theme. It is a reason, however, to avoid forcing a particular curricular area to "fit" the theme. In other cases there may be a curricular fit, yet a reluctant teacher. Nothing turns a teacher off from making connections in the curriculum quicker than being forced into doing it; simply move on with the theme without that individual's participation. Include those teachers as much as they want, and perhaps they will participate the next time around on a limited basis. Here, too, is an opportunity for the principal to encourage all teachers to become involved.

In curriculum integration, learning is approached in a more holistic way for students and teachers. With the theme as the organizing center, teachers discuss what knowledge, experiences, and insights they can bring to the learning experience, not based on their content expertise, but on the totality of their knowledge and skills. Subject boundaries dissolve with such units, as do the subject affiliations for teachers. For example, Mr. Smith is no longer viewed as the math teacher but as the teacher who guides students in their understanding of statistical analysis or in writing summary findings.

In the initial phases of any curriculum work, principals must provide the support that is essential for a thematic unit to be successful. Some teachers can successfully navigate the initial stages of involving students in the development of curriculum without the principal's support, but the enthusiasm for this worthwhile endeavor can quickly be dampened without key support from the administration.

What Principals Can Do To Support Their Teachers

☐ *Find time.* Make time for teachers to meet, plan, and begin working through the start-up process. Show your support by making time for reading, planning, and visiting similar programs.

☐ *Find resources.* There are pockets of teachers involved in various stages of curriculum integration across the country, and many of their stories are available in the literature. It is important for teachers embarking on this adventure to realize they don't have to reinvent this process. In addition to the printed resources available through National Middle School Association (see pp. 45-46) and elsewhere, principals should find teachers experienced with curriculum integration who will share their stories. This may very well be the best way a principal can help teachers interested in this approach.

☐ *Pave the way.* Work with central office personnel, and educate district leaders on curriculum integration. This works best over a period of time, sharing information and answering questions before they arise. In most districts, paving the way extends to include community and school board presentations.

☐ *Maintain a supportive school climate.* In almost all cases, curriculum integration begins with a team, not with the entire faculty. Some teachers are fearful that they will be expected to implement curriculum integration and therefore may attempt to undermine the work of those engaged in it initially. Others may resent any perceived benefits that the initial team might receive, such as attending conferences or school visits. Communicate early, openly, and often with the entire faculty to avoid petty jealousies and undermining efforts.

☐ *Communicate with parents.* Communicating with parents is essential. The best way to communicate is to show parents what and how their children are learning. Bring parents in to see demonstrations of their children working or planning curriculum. Don't spend a lot of time explaining how curriculum integration is different from traditional classrooms, but focus instead on demonstrating how much students are acquiring knowledge and skills and are actively and enthusiastically engaged in learning. Some schools offer parents the option of choosing the integrated curriculum team.

QUESTIONS TO CONSIDER

- How do you use the curriculum recommendations from *This We Believe: Successful Schools for Young Adolescents* as the basis for curriculum conversations in your school? (e.g. How is your curriculum relevant? challenging? integrative? exploratory?

- What kind of forums are in place to discuss curriculum issues?

- What is the plan in your school for making the curriculum more age appropriate for young adolescent students?

- What are the existing non-negotiable curriculum norms?

- To what extent do teachers know your beliefs, as principal, about various curriculum issues? What do you know about the curricular positions of your teams—and individual teachers?

Teaming Supports Curriculum Integration

*The good news is that great minds don't think alike. . . .We believe
the best ideas come from a room full of differing opinions.*
—*The Economist*

A major component of any successful middle level school is interdisciplinary teaming. Most commonly, teams include representatives of the core subjects: mathematics, language arts, science, and social studies, and sometimes a reading teacher, with each teaching his or her separate subject. While it is possible to develop integrated curriculum with a team of four or five teachers, it is far less likely than on a smaller partner team or one consisting of three teachers. Teachers prepared as content specialists often find it more difficult to organize curriculum by theme and focus on the totality of the learning experience called for in curriculum integration. Planning collaboratively with three or four other teachers, each with his or her own specialized training, is very difficult. Teams struggle with varied beliefs about the importance of connected curriculum and the role of student voice in the process. All of these factors make implementing an integrated curriculum a task calling for dedicated risk takers.

Smaller teams are more likely comprised of teachers with elementary or more generalized preparation. Due to their broad expertise, they often make connections between subject areas with greater ease. It is generally easier for two or three teacher teams to share a common teaching philosophy as well as the same expectations for day-to-day practices, compared to larger teams.

How does a principal encourage teams to get started on the journey toward integrated curriculum? Begin with a team committed to making connections across subjects and a desire to involve its students more actively in their own learning. These teachers see beyond isolated standards and standardized assessments. They are dissatisfied with traditional practices, which they recognize do not meet students' needs. They are concerned about the level of frustration many students exhibit with a disconnected curriculum and view curriculum integration as a way to engage more students and bring greater relevancy to the classroom. Teachers are more likely to try integrated curriculum when they have successfully used interdisciplinary units and have seen their students' depth of understanding grow. These teachers have a full grasp of the curriculum, instruction, and assessment learning process. They are thinkers, confident in their abilities, and often are seen by their peers as top-notch educators.

The principal must provide structure and many types of support for teachers who are venturing into curriculum integration. The principal must run interference with other teachers who are afraid the example of this team will mean they too will have to work this hard. The principal must work with the central office and school board to build support for these teachers when they are confronted by external questioning. Ultimately, the principal must be the curriculum integration team's greatest supporter. In schools where teams use integrated curriculum, the principal's support is the key to successfully implementing and maintaining this approach.

It is not surprising to find that teams engaging in this work are made up of over-achievers. That is how they come to this work in the first place. They are insightful, professional educators whose commitment to students is unmistakable. Their success in working with students and parents often influences other teams to step up their performance as well. As a team achieves more success with curriculum integration, administrators sometimes make the mistake of breaking up the team in order to jump-start other teams. This idea may have merit, but it often kills enthusiasm on a successful team, adds to burnout, and stifles growth. However, there are some circumstances where success can breed success, and team members placed on different teams can have a great influence on their new teams. Team members should always be consulted before changes are made in team composition, and their recommendations should be heeded in most cases. Dividing a team, especially early in the team's tenure, typically has a detrimental effect far outweighing the positive impact of assisting other teams.

A team can begin to structure its second year based on what was learned during the first year about planning with students, communicating with parents, implementing effective teaching strategies, and assessing using a more performance-based approach. This evaluation and reflection makes the team even more effective the second year, builds greater confidence, and given the right circumstances, begins to establish greater credibility within the school and community. Some believe a team does not reach its apex until the fifth year.

To spread the word about curriculum integration, encourage teachers to talk with, observe, and collaborate with the pioneering team and then slowly initiate the process themselves, bringing their own voices and personality to their team—not simply replicating the work of another team. The ownership is greater and outcomes typically more powerful when this happens.

Principals who fully support this work walk a fine line. It is possible to unabashedly support integrated curriculum and democratic classrooms while still supporting other good instructional practices by other teachers in the school. But principals must be clear in their vision and support and not denigrate other teams, helping all teams to work toward curriculum integration and involving students more in the learning process, regardless of where the teams are currently on the curriculum continuum.

Scheduling

A key structural feature of exemplary middle level schools is a flexible schedule where teachers have nearly total control over the block of time with their students so they can accommodate varied learning experiences. While certain elements of the daily schedule are not flexible—starting and dismissal times and lunch—given a flexible schedule, teams of teachers have the ability to adjust the time segments and the student groupings to match learning objectives, instead of trying to match learning experiences to an arbitrary bell schedule. To support integrated curriculum, a team needs large blocks of uninterrupted time to carry out various activities for students. In some of the most successful integrated environments, teams have students for up to four periods without interruption. Students do not leave the team during this time, and teachers are able to group and regroup students based on activities supporting the integrated unit of study.

In recent years more middle schools have embraced the high school form of block scheduling. Such block scheduling usually provides double periods for two subjects but perpetuates the separate subject approach. Students and teachers can engage in integrated curriculum with a wide variety of schedules including block schedules, rotating schedules, as well as alternate day schedules; however, the ideal schedule for integrated curriculum is simply large blocks of uninterrupted time. In that time, the team is free to schedule so that students can focus on large projects and engage in complex thinking—activities that are at the core of integrated classrooms.

Selecting Teachers for Curriculum Integration

Are curriculum integration and democratic classrooms for every teacher? There is no checklist or recipe for finding a teacher who is perfect for creating an integrated classroom. There are, however, some characteristics that are more commonly found in teachers who engage in this work, but these characteristics should not limit the thinking of a principal who seeks out like-minded educators. Some common characteristics beyond the pedagogical and content knowledge expected of all master teachers are that they

- View student failure as teacher failure
- Place great importance on students' processing their learning
- Share ownership of the classroom with students
- Understand and appreciate the natural inquisitiveness of young adolescents and can focus that trait to deepen learning experiences
- Create an invitational climate in their classrooms
- Develop an understanding of students as individuals and know their students well
- Envision themselves as significantly influencing student learning
- Feel good about themselves and their role as teachers
- Model positive self-esteem.

There are teachers in every school who in some way or another demonstrate these characteristics, and other teachers, for whatever reason, who have yet to exhibit these characteristics in their professional practices. One of the least talked about, yet most positive aspects of integrated curriculum is its power to change teachers' attitudes, beliefs, and practices. Time after time, teachers, who would not have given this approach a second thought, find themselves warming to the idea of democratic classrooms after viewing their colleagues and students engaged in this type of learning. Seasoned veterans who were counting the days or years to retirement gain their second wind and continue to teach for more years, commenting that using integrated curriculum in a democratic classroom is the most fun and professionally rewarding experience they have enjoyed in their teaching careers. These teachers often speak of deeper fulfillment in their work while acknowledging this instructional approach took a greater commitment of time. It is incumbent for middle level principals to expose all staff members to this approach, allow time for teachers to share with each other and observe classrooms where curriculum integration is in place and working well. Teachers have more credibility with their colleagues than any other group. They see their peers working with the same kinds of students and sharing the same kinds of resources, all in the same school environment. Teachers see their colleagues as non-threatening resources, accessible and able to provide "just in time" information when it is needed. Principals who effectively promote curriculum integration know the value of and foster these professional relationships.

Special Student Populations

Students in a democratic classroom where curriculum integration is used are in a learning environment that best matches their developmental status. This is the type of classroom most young adolescents will excel in and includes many who feel disenfranchised in regular classrooms, particularly special education and gifted and talented students. Because student voice is valued so highly in democratic classrooms, students previously frustrated by a lack of curriculum relevancy and unchallenged by tasks that require minimal thinking will thrive in this more engaging and stimulating learning environment. Typically, special education and gifted students make up a disproportionate number of those students who have disengaged from their daily learning experiences. Such students may be reinvigorated by a democratic classroom where curriculum integration is practiced.

Since these students experience greater success in democratic, integrated classrooms, principals often mistakenly assign a higher number of these students to these teams. Democratic, integrated classrooms should reflect the school's population—a heterogeneous grouping of all students. Assigning students in a manner that does not truly reflect the overall population of the school can create a climate that impedes student learning—and should be avoided. The integrated curriculum is meant for all students; it is the general education experience that is most age appropriate for young adolescents, and principals should work diligently to achieve this type of classroom for all students.

QUESTIONS TO CONSIDER

- How does the existing team structure promote collaboration?
- How do teams use common planning time regularly to make connections across the curriculum?
- Are the sizes of teams conducive to creating small learning communities and engaging in curriculum integration?
- Do team members have similar beliefs about student learning and creating effective classroom environments?
- How does the schedule provide adequate common planning time for teachers to discuss curriculum, conduct team business, and meet with students or parents?
- How does the schedule provide large blocks of time under the direction of the teaching team to support a variety of learning activities for students?
- How does the schedule provide the team with flexibility to group and regroup students for various learning activities? To what extent do teams take advantage of this opportunity?
- Are students grouped heterogeneously, and do they represent the unique mix of the entire school?

TOPIC FIVE

Standards Support Curriculum Integration

The promise of the "standards movement" for better learning and teaching lies in embracing new norms and routines that can turn schools into places that celebrate all kinds of accomplishments, where it is both desirable and safe for every student to become smart, work hard, and learn through risk taking and effort.
            —Anne Wheelock

The standards movement has been growing in importance and has definitely impacted middle level educators and students during the past decade. From early national content standards, first released by the National Council of Teachers of Mathematics in 1989 (NCTM, 1989), to more recently adopted state standards in all 50 states (Reeves, 2004), content standards have brought a different focus and a higher level of accountability to classrooms across the country. Unfortunately for many dedicated middle level educators, the standards movement has also helped reverse the trend toward more integrated curriculum and democratic classrooms, often sending the curriculum back to a single subject approach with little or no attempt to connect with other subjects.

The question middle level educators must ask now is: *Can integrated curriculum really work in a content-driven, standards-based, high-accountability environment?* The answer is yes! Integrating curriculum was never described as an easy task for middle level educators, and the standards movement has not made the process any easier. However, even with the most specific content standards, integrated curriculum can thrive (Beane & Vars, 2000).

In classrooms where teachers are responsible for developing themes, integrated curriculum can emerge from extensive curriculum mapping. Here, teachers use their planning time to make connections between the various content areas and use age-appropriate themes to frame questions to be answered during the integrated unit. This can take considerable time, especially for larger teams. It can also be difficult for teachers to pull content from a single subject unit they have used for years and connect portions of that content to completely different integrated units of study. But it can be done, creating a cohesive unit of age-appropriate content revolving around a connecting theme.

One argument some educators use to avoid integrating the curriculum is the inordinate number of standards they are expected to teach. How, they question, can they get involved in an integrated unit and still teach all the content required? Many educators have found that integrated curriculum can actually provide them with more time. As teachers map the curriculum, overlapping content and skills becomes more obvious. Skills are positioned in the appropriate place in the curriculum and taught once when they are needed in a functional context, rather than repeatedly taught in an ineffective, isolated fashion.

It would seem that prescribed standards by state educational agencies run counter to a curriculum based on the questions and concerns young adolescents have about themselves and their world. Standards certainly have made the process more complex for educators, yet it is still possible for middle level educators to design a standards-based curriculum around the topics generated by middle level students through the process of "back loading." Middle level teachers, using a yearlong planning model, ask students to list questions and concerns they have about themselves and their world. Common questions and concerns emerge from students, creating their organizing themes for the school year. Educators then "back load" the standards into the organizing themes. The themes that came from students' questions and concerns become standards based. The students themselves become familiar with state and national standards and learn to identify and place standards accordingly.

There will be some standards that do not logically fit with a theme. These standards should not be forced into an existing theme nor should they be ignored. These standards can be taught as "givens" in an appropriate subject and also incorporate students' input in presenting this isolated content. Skilled teachers can move fluidly from an integrated curriculum to separate subject teaching and guide students in forming questions that reflect their concerns.

Steps in Using Content Standards to Plan an Integrated Unit of Study

☐ *Commit to ample time for planning.* Trying to implement an integrated unit that has been hastily constructed will frustrate teachers and inhibit optimal effectiveness with students. It is better to do one well-developed integrated unit than do two or three quickly constructed units that leave teachers feeling overwhelmed and students not fully understanding the range of connections made in the unit.

☐ *Understand the standards.* It may seem like a simple thing, but having teachers well versed in the standards will assist them in making the connections between the various subject areas. A first-year educator will not likely possess the content expertise and experience to make the curriculum connections. However, inexperienced teachers can join with veteran teachers in teaching the standards by reviewing and becoming thoroughly familiar with them. Likewise team members with experience in integrated curriculum will bring needed insights.

☐ *Design the unit with age-appropriate learning outcomes based on topics relevant to young adolescents.* This is an area where many units get stalled or take a turn for the worse. The unit should be organized around a theme that is appropriate for young adolescents, not a "cute" theme, a theme a teacher particularly likes, or one driven by a great activity or fun field trip. As educators examine the content standards, what learning outcomes are evident for students? What assessment activities can show teachers that students not only understand the content, but can apply it as well? Do these assessment activities fragment the curriculum or strengthen the connections?

Common Pitfalls

Those experienced in designing integrated curriculum experiences with students have identified some common pitfalls when undertaking this type of work. Watch out for these potential problems:

☐ *Meeting the deadline.* Teams often are encouraged, sometimes required, to commit to one themed unit each semester. While this timeline can push some teams forward, it is important that teams have time to fully plan each unit before implementing it.

☐ *The unit gets too large.* Instead of designing a relevant, focused integrated unit, a theme unit can grow to 12-weeks or longer and exhaust both teachers and students. A short, successful unit will do more to ensure future attempts than a long, disconnected unit. Think big, start small.

☐ *Forcing everyone to participate.* Especially on larger teams, there is often the expectation that everyone must participate in the unit from beginning to end. There are some cases when this is possible, especially for smaller, well-established teams; but with first efforts, some teachers may not see adequate connections or only see connections for a portion of the unit. A science teacher, for example, may only be involved for one week of a three-week unit. Do not force teachers who do not wish to participate in the unit, although it is important they are part of the planning to see how the process works. Chances are good they will participate, perhaps in a limited fashion on a future unit, once they see the success of this unit. Additionally, forcing someone to "stretch his or her content" for the length of the unit is not a good idea. In a standards-based environment, time is especially precious; spending additional time to meet the parameters of the unit when the content can be effectively taught in a shorter period of time is frustrating and may cause some teachers to avoid future opportunities with curriculum integration.

☐ *Inadequate processing and reflection.* One of the most neglected, yet most important aspects of completing an integrated unit is the process that follows. Successful teachers always engage in reflective practice. Teams of teachers should take time to review successes and identify needed changes following a unit of study. Student feedback is critical and should be solicited.

QUESTIONS TO CONSIDER

- How can state and district content standards be structured locally to promote curriculum integration?
- Do teachers have adequate planning time to coordinate standards with themes that emerge from students' questions and concerns about themselves and the world around them? Do they use it effectively?
- How can learning outcomes specified in the standards be met through an integrated curriculum?

Professional Development

Only the wisest and stupidest people never change.—Confucius

Some educational leaders, anxious to implement this approach, will ask for a map leading the way to curriculum integration. In reality, there is no map, just a compass that points in the general direction. The ideas in this resource are gleaned from educators across the country who committed to integrated curriculum. Much of what they have learned has come through trial and error from years of working with young adolescents—and teachers.

Principals need to consider what types of professional development activities they can use to move their teachers toward more integrated, democratic classrooms. There is no step-by-step list to follow; and it is not safe to assume that teachers, teams, or faculties are at the same level professionally and philosophically. There are, however, some common tendencies that may indicate a team or group of teachers is ready to move toward a more integrated curriculum. Keep your eyes open for these positive signs:

☐ *Successful multidisciplinary units.* An established team tries a multidisciplinary unit: team members work together to coordinate and compact the curriculum; they define common scoring rubrics and often collaborate on assignments allowing a project or other assignment to receive credit in more than one class. Such a team may be ready to move forward when given encouragement. While successful multidisciplinary units are often positive first steps toward a more integrated curriculum, many teams stop at this level and never move ahead to true curriculum integration. They may lack vision or confidence and need the assistance of the principal to help them take the next steps.

☐ **_Evidence of dissolving disciplinary boundaries_**. As a team works together over time, teachers shift content and assignments among classes seamlessly. The social studies teacher may work with students on a writing assignment, while the math and science teachers collaborate on a charting and graphing assignment or data analysis. In these situations student learning becomes more important than content affiliation and that may open for attempting curriculum integration.

☐ **_Flexible use of time or multitasking occurs._** When teachers frequently juggle the schedule to better match learning activities in available time frames, it appears they might be ready for using an integrative approach. New learning activities are organized flexibly on the team, and all students are not doing the same thing at the same time. Students are frequently grouped and regrouped based on their interests and the learning task, and almost always heterogeneously.

☐ **_Student involvement is evident._** Gauging the level of student involvement in a classroom may take some time and some dialogue with students, but will provide a level of readiness for moving into integrated curriculum. Are students given assignment choices? Do students share ideas on possible assignments and work with the teacher to define the assessment criteria? Are the opinions of all students valued, or are only those students who move quickly through the content allowed to share ideas? Suggesting more input into curriculum planning by students will make perfect sense to teachers ready to design a more integrated curriculum in democratic classrooms.

Teachers who display such practices would appear to be ready to move toward more integrated classrooms. Principals should then talk with these teachers, share resources, and encourage them to cross disciplinary boundaries. Frequently, good classroom teachers will seek out the building principal for support to move their classrooms toward a more integrated curriculum model, but a principal should not wait for those teachers to step forward on their own.

Principals who want to move from an occasional multidisciplinary unit to more fully integrated classrooms should think big and start small. The vast majority of teachers and teams using integrated curriculum today started off on a small scale and gained experience before moving to a yearlong integrated curriculum model. The initial abbreviated experience provided a source of encouragement, support, and information, while the smaller scale approach also better confined missteps that are bound to happen. Even the best ideas can be implemented poorly, and a small-scale approach allows time for refinement—and readjustment—and helps ensure future success.

QUESTIONS TO CONSIDER

- When and where do your teachers engage in professional practice dialogues?
- How frequent are opportunities for teachers to share their curriculum and instructional practices?
- How do teachers ask critical questions and provide constructive feedback to their colleagues as a part of using "Looking at Student Work" protocols?
- How does your professional development plan include support for a curriculum integration focus?

TOPIC SEVEN

Creating Positive Public Relations

Only those who dare to fail greatly can ever achieve greatly.
— Robert Kennedy

The success or failure of curriculum integration in many middle schools is not a result of what actually takes place in the classroom but rather the public relations—or lack thereof—that take place outside the classroom. The principal is key to creating positive relationships that better ensure the success of curriculum integration and enhanced student learning. Principals are accustomed to talking positively about their schools and trumpeting successes. They understand the importance of creating positive public relations, whereas classroom teachers are likely to be less adept at this function. Principals skilled in positive public relations, then, should have a plan for sharing information about curriculum integration with their own faculty and staff, central office personnel, school board, parents, and the school community.

Principals, especially those who have been involved in the school for any length of time, know the culture of the community and their receptiveness to changes in practices and programs. The type and amount of communication needed are impacted by this knowledge and the depth of change as a result of implementing integrated curriculum. Defining how the scope of change will impact the school community is essential since it will drive the communications plan. For example, a team of teachers engaged in a two-week integrated unit of study will typically need to communicate with a much smaller audience, typically parents, possibly school staff, and central office personnel, than a team of teachers planning to launch a yearlong integrated program.

Critical Talking Points for Curriculum Integration

☐ Make clear that the state standards will still be taught in an integrated approach—how teachers teach the standards and connect them may be different in an integrated classroom, but the state standards for students in this grade or class will still be met. In cases where they have been overly scrutinized in preparation for an integrated unit, teachers should list all the state standards that will be incorporated in the integrated unit.

☐ Student learning outcomes, based on the state standards, will be at least as rigorous as those expected in subject-focused classes. This point should be made up front. For example if students were to complete a 750-word narrative essay in English class, the expectation is that they would complete a 750-word narrative essay in the classroom where curriculum is integrated.

☐ Provide specific examples of student work from past units that demonstrate how state standards were met. Student work is a powerful indicator of the rigor of integrated curriculum. Viewing the types of in-depth demonstrations of student learning, typically far exceeding what takes place in subject-centered classrooms, often puts those skeptical about this type of approach at ease. Always note that the focus should be on what students are learning—not how the curriculum is organized.

☐ Provide testimonials from former students and their parents to lend credibility to the program. Parents and school officials expect to hear positive comments from the teachers leading the program, but the most powerful spokespersons are those students who have participated in integrated units of study. People notice when parents talk about their child's not being fully challenged until he or she was in a classroom where curriculum integration was used, or when a student states that this approach was the most powerful school experience she ever had.

QUESTIONS TO CONSIDER

- What can you do to ensure that central office staff and school board members understand this curricular approach and support it?

- How will you deal with educators not engaged in this curricular approach who might sabotage those involved with it?

- What will you do to ensure that parents have sufficient understanding to explain curriculum integration to others—and promote it when necessary?

The trend to move beyond the separate subject approach for middle level schools has reached a level where interdisciplinary instruction is now an expectation, but few see this as the end. Supported by increasing examples from the field and research findings, efforts are underway in successful middle schools that are implementing an integrative curriculum approach that solicits student voice and leads to democratic classrooms. Remember, in nearly every middle level school there is usually at least one teacher or one team engaged in this kind of integrative work that students find so challenging, relevant, and stimulating.

Effective middle school principals need to be leaders in these efforts, not only by providing moral support but by taking the initiative in various ways to advance the implementation of this curriculum approach, which engages students and leads to greater, more long-lasting achievement.

References

Beane, J.A. (1993). *A middle school curriculum: From rhetoric to reality* (2nd ed.). Columbus, OH: National Middle School Association.

Beane, J.A. (2002) *Curriculum matters. Organizing the middle school curriculum.* Retrieved October 17, 2005, from http://www.nmsa.org

Beane, J., & Vars, G. (2000). *Integrative curriculum in a standards-based world.* ERIC document 441 618.

Jackson, A.W., & Davis, G.A. (2000). *Turning points 2000: Educating adolescents in the 21st century.* New York and Westerville, OH: Teachers College Press and National Middle School Association.

Kilpatrick, W. (1918). The project method. *Teachers College Record, 19,* 319-35.

National Council of Teachers of Mathematics. (1989). *Curriculum and evaluation standards for school mathematics.* Reston, VA: Author.

National Middle School Association. (2003). *This we believe: Successful schools for young adolescents.* Westerville, OH: Author

Reeves, D.A. (2004). Accountability for learning: *How teachers and school leaders can take charge.* Reston, VA: Association for Supervision and Curriculum Development.

Additional Resources on Integrated Curriculum from National Middle School Association

Watershed: A Successful Voyage into Integrative Learning,
by Mark Springer.

The dream of a fully integrative curriculum is achievable as chronicled by the author of this full-day, experiential program in which 40 motivated seventh graders use real-life activities and become responsible for their own education.

The Story of Alpha: A Multiage, Student-Centered Team—33 Years and Counting, by Susan Kuntz.

This volume chronicles the history of a middle grades team in Vermont that uses a multiage and multiyear classroom, integrated curriculum, and student-driven goal setting to truly set it apart from most other classrooms.

A Middle School Curriculum: From Rhetoric to Reality, by James A. Beane.

This book has initiated serious discussions about middle school curriculum and the limited effectiveness of subject-centered organization. It presents a student-centered approach that has become the model for a fully integrative curriculum.

Curriculum Integration: Twenty Questions–With Answers, by Gert Nesin and John Lounsbury.

Twenty of the most frequently asked questions about curriculum integration are answered in this resource for teachers and teams moving toward integrated curriculum. This book provides a strong rationale and encourages teachers to discover the benefits of kids becoming active participants in their own learning.

Academic Success Through Empowering Students, by Cathy Vatterott.

Student empowerment requires a solid understanding about the links between young adolescent development and learning. Examples of empowering classes and Web-based resources are included in this relevant resource.

Student-Oriented Curriculum: Asking the Right Questions, by
Wallace M. Alexander with Dennis Carr and Kathy McAvoy.

This is the story of two teachers and 40 sixth graders who
achieved success beyond their expectations by actively involving students
in all aspects of the teaching and learning process. Also included
are 16 lessons learned that will both encourage and guide middle level
educators.

***Safe To Be Smart: Building a Culture for Standards-Based Reform
in the Middle Grades,*** by Anne Wheelock.

This book deals fully and fairly with the complexity of implementing
standards in all classes for all students and makes it clear that
standards-based reform involves changing not simply the content of
learning but the standard operating procedures of schools.

Turning Points 2000: Educating Adolescents in the 21st Century, by
Anthony W. Jackson and Gayle A. Davis.

This book extends and elaborates on the recommendations of
the Carnegie Corporations's 1989 landmark report, *Turning Points:
Preparing American Youth for the 21st Century.* Particularly valuable
are chapters dealing with curriculum and assessment and designing
instruction.

*(To order these and other NMSA publications, call 1-800-528-6672
or visit our Web site at www.nmsa.org)*

National Middle School Association

National Middle School Association, established in 1973, is the voice for professionals and others interested in the education and well-being of young adolescents. The association has grown rapidly and enrolls members in all 50 states, the Canadian provinces, and 42 other nations. In addition, 58 state, regional, and provincial middle school associations are official affiliates of NMSA.

NMSA is the only national association dedicated exclusively to the education, development, and growth of young adolescents. Membership is open to all. While middle level teachers and administrators make up the bulk of the membership, central office personnel, college and university faculty, state department officials, other professionals, parents, and lay citizens are members and active in supporting our single mission—improving the educational experiences of 10- to 15-year-olds. This open and diverse membership is a particular strength of NMSA's.

The association publishes *Middle School Journal*, the movement's premier professional journal; *Research in Middle Level Education Online*; *Middle Ground, the Magazine of Middle Level Education; Family Connection,* an online newsletter for families; *Classroom Connections,* a practical quarterly resource; and a series of research summaries.

A leading publisher of professional books and monographs in the field of middle level education, NMSA provides resources both for understanding and advancing various aspects of the middle school concept and for assisting classroom teachers in planning for instruction. More than 70 NMSA publications as well as selected titles published by other organizations are available through the resource catalog .

The association's highly acclaimed annual conference has drawn many thousands of registrants every fall. NMSA also sponsors many other professional development opportunities.

For information about NMSA and its many services, contact the association's headquarters office at 4151 Executive Parkway, Suite 300, Westerville, Ohio, 43081. TELEPHONE: 800-528-NMSA; FAX: 614-895-4750; INTERNET: www. nmsa.org.